D0835571

THE BEST OF
BRITISH COMEDY

Only Fools
and Horses

In the same series:

THE BEST OF
BRITISH COMEDY

*Only Fools
and Horses*

THE BEST SCENES, JOKES AND ONE-LINERS

Richard Webber

HarperCollins*Publishers*

HarperCollins*Publishers*
77–85 Fulham Palace Road,
Hammersmith, London W6 8JB
www.harpercollins.co.uk

First published by HarperCollins*Publishers* 2009

1

A catalogue record of this book
is available from the British Library

ISBN 978-0-00-731896-4

Printed and bound in China
by Leo Paper Products Ltd

ACKNOWLEDGEMENTS

I'm grateful, once again, to John Sullivan for allowing me to include script extracts and for giving up more time to chat about *Only Fools and Horses*. Thanks, also, to John Challis, Sue Holderness, Roger Lloyd Pack and Paul Barber and all the other actors who were willing to chat. Finally, thanks to my agent Jeffrey Simmons.

EPISODE LIST

Series One

Christmas Special

Series Two

1. 'The Long Legs Of The Law' (21/10/82)
2. 'Ashes To Ashes' (28/10/82)
3. 'A Losing Streak' (4/11/82)
4. 'No Greater Love ...' (11/11/82)
5. 'The Yellow Peril' (18/11/82)
6. 'It Never Rains ...' (25/11/82)
7. 'A Touch Of Glass' (2/12/82)

Christmas Special

'The Funny Side Of Christmas: Christmas Trees'
(27/12/82)

Christmas Special

'Diamonds Are For Heather' (30/12/82)

Series Three

1. 'Homesick' (10/11/83)
2. 'Healthy Competition' (17/11/83)
3. 'Friday The 14th' (24/11/83)
4. 'Yesterday Never Comes' (1/12/83)

Series Five

1. 'From Prussia With Love' (31/8/86)
2. 'The Miracle Of Peckham' (7/9/86)
3. 'The Longest Night' (14/9/86)
4. 'Tea For Three' (21/9/86)
5. 'Video Nasty' (28/9/86)
6. 'Who Wants To Be A Millionaire' (5/10/86)

Christmas Special

'A Royal Flush' (25/12/86)

Christmas Special

'The Frog's Legacy' (25/12/87)

Christmas Special

'Dates' (25/12/88)

Series Six

1. 'Yuppy Love' (8/1/89)
2. 'Danger UXD' (15/1/89)

3. 'Chain Gang' (22/1/89)
4. 'The Unlucky Winner Is …' (29/1/89)
5. 'Sickness and Wealth' (5/2/89)
6. 'Little Problems' (12/2/89)

Christmas Special

'The Jolly Boys' Outing' (25/12/89)

Christmas Special

'Rodney Come Home' (25/12/90)

Series Seven

1. 'The Sky's The Limit' (30/12/90)
2. 'The Chance Of A Lunchtime' (6/1/91)
3. 'Stage Fright' (13/1/91)
4. 'The Class Of '62' (20/1/91)
5. 'He Ain't Heavy, He's My Uncle' (27/1/91)
6. 'Three Men, A Woman And A Baby' (3/2/91)

Christmas Special

1. 'Miami Twice – Part One: The American Dream' (24/12/91)
2. 'Miami Twice – Part Two: Oh To Be In England' (25/12/91)

Christmas Special

'Mother Nature's Son' (25/12/92)

Christmas Special

'Fatal Extraction' (25/12/93)

Christmas Trilogy

1. 'Heroes And Villains' (25/12/96)
2. 'Modern Men' (27/12/96)
3. 'Time On Our Hands' (29/12/96)

Comic Relief Special

(14/3/97)

Christmas Special

'If They Could See Us Now …!' (25/12/01)

Christmas Special

'Strangers On The Shore' (25/12/02)

Christmas Special

'Sleepless In Peckham' (25/12/03)

INTRODUCTION

Not many sitcoms succeed in ingraining themselves into the British psyche, but *Only Fools and Horses*, written by the unassuming John Sullivan, whose other success stories include *Just Good Friends*, *Citizen Smith*, *Dear John* and, of course, *Green, Green, Grass*, did just that.

During its 23-year run, 64 episodes were shown, with the lion's share attracting sizeable audience figures. Topping the

'CREME DE LA MENTHE.' (DEL)

list, 'Time On Our Hands', the final instalment in 1996's Christmas Trilogy, pulled in a whopping 24.3 million viewers.

As always, many factors lay behind the show's indubitable success, including John Sullivan's ability to evince a sense of realism into the scripts, confidently blending seriousness with the comedy oozing from every episode. Undoubtedly, *Only*

Fools was a rich study of people's foibles and life's issues. John wasn't scared to confront tough subjects in his work. What less talented scriptwriters might have shied away from, he faced head-on: miscarriage, impotence, fraud, violence, death – just some of the delicate topics spotlighted in his well-loved sitcom.

Here, in a similar style to the two previous books in the series, celebrating *Dad's Army* and *Porridge*, we bring you a host of well-crafted, perfectly honed scenes; uproarious one-liners; revealing insights from not only John Sullivan but the actors as well; an overview of the sitcom's life and a barrow load of other goodies, too. As Del would put it, it's all lovely jubbly!

RICHARD WEBBER

THE STORY IN A NUTSHELL

Writer John Sullivan had already scored with a hit sitcom, in the shape of Citizen Smith, by the time he turned his attention to Only Fools and Horses.

The then BBC head of entertainment, Jimmy Gilbert, had played a key role in launching Sullivan's writing career by commissioning *Citizen Smith* and was keen to retain the services of the talented writer. Although he wasn't enamoured of the title, *Only Fools and Horses*, he knew immediately that the sitcom's premise – a London family who wouldn't sponge off the state as they wheeled and dealed their way through life from one dubious business deal to the next – would work.

The first series was eventually commissioned, centred on the Trotter family, a surname Sullivan had encountered previously, having worked with someone of the same name.

Experienced director Ray Butt took control of the opening season before passing the reins on to Gareth Gwenlan.

When it came to casting, Nicholas Lyndhurst was already in the frame to play Rodney, a decision which pleased Sullivan. Finding his older brother was trickier. Enn Reitel and Jim

---

Did you know?

Only Fools and Horses was originally titled *Readies*. The name was eventually changed to the former, which had previously been used for an episode of *Citizen Smith*.

Broadbent were both considered before David Jason's name entered the frame. By chance, director Ray Butt watched a repeat of *Open All Hours*, with Jason playing Granville, and knew instantly that he'd found his man.

With Lennard Pearce recruited to play Grandad, the opening series kicked off with the episode 'Big Brother' on 8 September 1981. The six episodes comprising the first season didn't set the world alight in terms of audience figures, attracting just under eight million viewers. But this was the era

Del had no sense of style.

where new programmes were given time to find their feet in the over-subscribed world of TV.

Great writing and sublime acting were the fundamentals behind the success that followed; regarding the latter, the adroit casting which paired David Jason with Nicholas Lyndhurst couldn't have been more profitable. Jason's animated and overt portrayal of the older brother was juxtaposed by Lyndhurst's beautifully crafted interpretation of the languid younger Trotter.

Initially, John Sullivan didn't think the BBC were keen on the sitcom and half-expected it to be scrapped after the first season; he was, therefore, delighted when asked to pen a second series, although the average audience figures, just under nine million, were far from ideal. It wasn't until Series Four, which saw viewing numbers average above 14 million, that the show had found its footing. Sadly, though, the growing success paled into insignificance when the death of Lennard Pearce, alias Grandad, was announced. John Sullivan *et al* were left with a dilemma: how to bridge the almighty chasm left behind by Pearce's sudden death. Recasting was out of the question, so John – while meeting with Ray Butt and Gareth Gwenlan – suggested introducing Albert, Grandad's brother, to add an extra dimension. After frantic rewriting of the scripts, Uncle Albert made his first appearance attending his brother's

Rodney always felt he lived in his brother's shadow.

funeral in 'Strained Relations'. Buster Merryfield, a bank manager turned actor, was welcomed into the fold and delivered a sterling job under difficult circumstances.

By the time Series Six was screened, the episodes had been extended to 50 minutes and *Only Fools and Horses* had established itself as arguably the BBC's most popular programme. Extended episodes proved beneficial in many respects, including John Sullivan not having to cut funny

'OH THE EXTERMINATOR. WELL, OF COURSE, TO RODDERS THAT IS ROMANTIC. I MEAN, HE CRIED HIS LITTLE EYES OUT OVER THE TEXAS CHAINSAW MASSACRE.' (DEL)

scenes purely to reduce the length of the script and affording him the opportunity and time to explore his characters and storylines in more depth.

In the latter stages of the sitcom, we saw the Trotter brothers finally settle down and take on life's responsibilities more willingly. In due course, Del and Rodney discovered true love in the shape of Raquel – who was only expected to appear in one episode but made such an impact the character was retained – and Cassandra respectively, and, later, fatherhood. The Trotter brothers were maturing, settling down and discarding their lads-about-town image.

Although the boys' marriages suffered more than their fair share of ups and downs, again providing John Sullivan with the chance to exploit his skills of writing the poignant moments, the series had moved on to a more mature level.

All good things must come to an end, though, and the screening of the 1996 Christmas Trilogy marked the cessation of visits to the Trotter household – or so everybody thought. If this had been the end, the show certainly went out with a bang. Each of the three episodes were watched by over 20 million viewers with the final instalment, 'Time On Our Hands', with the Trotters finally becoming millionaires, pulling in a colossal 24.3 million viewers, all glued to their screens to bid farewell to Del, Rodney, Uncle Albert and the rest of the gang. As always, the episodes had successfully mixed pathos with humour, and it was clear the British public were going to miss catching up with the frustrating yet loveable Trotter boys.

When the brothers struck gold, it looked like the lights would be switched off at Nelson Mandela House for good. No one intended making more episodes, but in the world of TV you never say never. One day, a throwaway comment from Gareth Gwenlan, hinting that perhaps a special episode would be made to celebrate the new millennium, started the ball rolling and, eventually, they were back.

Turning his attention to the scripts, Sullivan knew that keeping the Trotters as multi-millionaires wouldn't have worked. If they were to stroll the streets of Peckham once again, he wanted to return them to where they started; the trouble was, he couldn't do that in one episode. Eventually, another trilogy was commissioned.

John Sullivan decided the Trotters would lose their fortune, thanks to Del gambling away their millions on the Central American money market, and so five years after the final instalment in the Christmas Trilogy, the crowd were back.

The three episodes, 'If They Could See Us Now …!', 'Strangers On The Shore' and 'Sleepless In Peckham' – and this time they would be the last – were transmitted on Christmas Day 2001, 2002 and 2003. There were times when Sullivan regretted writing the new shows because the press reaction was disappointing, despite winning plaudits from the audiences. Later, though, John was able to appreciate the episodes which, again, proved that quality writing, casting and acting win every time.

'BIG BROTHER'

The Trotter brothers have a meeting at midday and Rodney is far from ready. Del is horrified to discover the reason why.

DEL: (*Studying his reflection in the mirror*) S'il vous plait, s'il vous plait, what an enigma. I get better looking every day. I can't wait for tomorrow. Oh, do you know, I'm suffering from something incurable. (*Grandad and Rodney ignore him*) Still, never mind, eh! Oi, come on Rodney, shake a leg, we've got a meeting at 12. What are you doing?

RODNEY: Our accounts.

DEL: You keeping accounts now? Well there you are, Grandad, a lot of people told me I was a right dipstick to make my brother a partner in the business, but this only goes to prove how

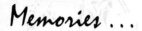

Memories ...

'Nick and Lennard were great to work with. Although he was very young, Nick had spent his entire life, more or less, in the business because he'd been a child actor. Lennard Pearce, meanwhile, had been a stage actor for all his life. So we were dealing with actors who I had a healthy respect for because they had served their apprenticeship.

'Both of them were tremendously easy to get on with, but I think a lot of that was because we'd all worked a lot of time in the theatre, travelling the country, working every night with a live audience, learning our trade. That is hugely beneficial when you work in television. So with John Sullivan's scripts, and the experience of the cast, I knew we had the essential ingredients.'

DAVID JASON

bloody right they were. You dozy little twonk, Rodney, this is prima-facie evidence ain't it? The taxman gets hold of that he'll put us away for three years.

Raise your glasses to over two decades of sitcom success.

Rodney thinks Del is cheating him … the trouble is, he can't prove it.

RODNEY: It's obvious you're stitching me up. Look at you, you have three or four changes of clothes a day. Me – I've got one suit from the Almost New Shop. It gets embarrassing sometimes.

DEL: Oh, I embarrass you do I? You've got room to talk. You have been nothing but an embarrassment to me from the moment you was born. You couldn't be like any other little brother could you, and come along a couple of years after me. Oh no, you had to wait 13 years. So while all the other Mods were having punch-ups down at Southend and going to Who concerts, I was at home baby-sitting! I could never get your oystermilk stains out of me Ben Shermans – I used to find rusks in me Hush Puppies.

'GO WEST YOUNG MAN'

Del and Rodney try chatting up girls at a nightclub. The trouble is, Del reverts to a pack of lies, suggesting his younger brother is an international tennis player, in order to impress but, as usual, just makes a fool of himself.

DEL: Yeah, he's an international professional tennis player and I'm his manager. You must have heard of Rodney, yeah Rodney. The sporting press call him Hot Rod!

NICKY: Don't think I have. What's the surname?

'WHAT A PLONKER!' (DEL)

RODNEY: Trotter!

NICKY: Doesn't ring a bell, sorry.

15

DEL: No, no that's because we generally concentrate on the big American tournaments, you see.

MICHELE: Do you ever play Wimbledon?

DEL: No, no, we only play the big 'uns! We've just come back from the Miami Open …

NICKY: Really? You're not very tanned for Miami, are you?

RODNEY: No, no, it was an indoor tournament.

Did you know?
Offers to turn *Only Fools* into a film and stage production have been made over the years.

DEL: Yeah, yeah, it's amazing that, innit. I mean they call it the Miami Open and then they go an' hold it indoors. That's the Yanks for yer though eh? Anyway, we can't complain like because he won it, he did, he er, beat that Jimmy Connolly in the final.

MICHELE: Jimmy Connelly? Don't you mean Jimmy Connors?

16

Memories ...

'When I began writing *Only Fools* I never had a system of working. I've had mobiles by the side of my bed, Dictaphones, but when the ideas happen, they just happen.

'Initially, I wrote *Fools* straight on to an old-fashioned typewriter. Then, slowly, I turned to computers. But during the days of the typewriter, I'd sometimes work through the night re-typing.

'I change my scripts and mess about with them so much before putting "first draft" on it. By then, I've actually changed it six or seven times. In these early stages, it's like weaning a baby, but eventually I can get quite nasty with my script.

'Once we're in the editing suite, I don't care about favourite lines. When I started, Dennis Main Wilson gave me the best advice: "Never fall in love with your lines." He was right because that can cause you such pain.'

JOHN SULLIVAN

DEL: No, he knocked that didlio out in the first round, nine sets to one! Actually we're only in London to get Hot Rod here measured up for a new bat.

'TRES BIEN ENSEMBLE.' (DEL)

MICHELE: It's a racquet!

DEL: It is, the price they charge, darling.

'THE SECOND TIME AROUND'

Street traders Del and Rodney are using their sales patter, trying desperately to shift packs of hankies from a suitcase, surrounded by a crowd of women shoppers.

DEL: Here we are, the finest French lace hankies – there you are, they're a pleasure to have the flu with! Thanks, luv.

RODNEY: Now, hurry up girls, get in while the going's good. It's one for the price of two. One for the price of two.

DEL: Keep taking the money, Rodney, I'm gonna pop down the pub to get a lemonade for the old Hobsons.

RODNEY: Get us a packet of pork scratchings would you?

DEL: Pork scratchings. Sounds like a pig with fleas.

RODNEY: Come on then, get in while the going's good. We're not here today gone tomorrow, we're here today gone this afternoon, now come on.

....

Rodney and Grandad aren't happy when Del starts dating his scheming, money-grabbing ex-fiancée again, especially when they get engaged once more and she moves in.

DEL: (*Looking at Grandad*) What's up with you then, eh?

GRANDAD: It's her innit!

DEL: What?

GRANDAD: She's hid my teeth!

DEL: What? What you hidden his teeth for then, petal?

PAULINE: Look you don't know what it's like in this place. You and Rodney are out at the auctions or the market. But I'm stuck here with him. He's nibbling all day long. There'd be nothing left if I let him carry on! Don't worry, he gets his teeth back at meal times.

Lennard Pearce was a key factor in the show's success.

Rodney and Grandad, fed up with Del reigniting his flame for ex-fiancée Pauline, state they're leaving and forming their own partnership. Unable to believe what he's hearing, Del thinks Rodney is off his rocker.

DEL: A partnership! A partnership, you and Grandad? Gawd leave it out, Rodney, what have you been doing, sitting on your brains again? You must have noticed at some time or another that he doesn't move. You know he made the front page of the *Lancet*, don't you, as being the only living man in history to be treated for rigor mortis.

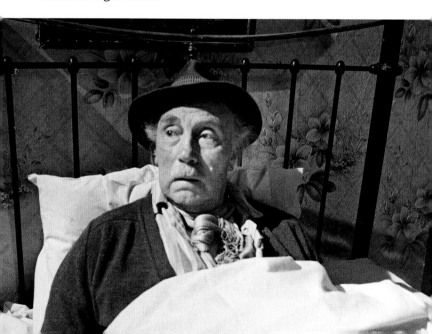

'THE RUSSIANS ARE COMING'

The Trotters are holed up in a do-it-yourself nuclear fallout shelter, after they stumble across the contraption and Rodney believes they should save themselves from the bomb.

DEL: (*To Rodney*) Here, here Oppenheimer, listen, if the bomb was to drop round here, how long would we have to stay inside this thing here?

RODNEY: Well, it depends upon the degree of the contamination in the air outside. 'Cos we're in a very vulnerable position here being close to the docks. But I would say roughly – give or take a week or two – about … two years!

DEL/GRANDAD: Two years?

RODNEY: Yeah, give or take a week or two.

DEL: If you think I'm staying in a lead-lined Nissan hut with you and Grandad and a chemical bloody khazi you've got another think coming.

RODNEY: Yeah, but if we leave the shelter within two years we'd die of radiation poisoning.

DEL: And if we stay inside the shelter for two years we'll die of bloody lead poisoning.

GRANDAD: He's right, Rodney. The rescue team will whip us straight round the nearest scrap metal yard.

Memories . . .

'The whole idea of "The Russians Are Coming" started when I worked for the council. We were sent to shift stuff from a demolished place and found lots of valuable lead. We wondered what it had been used for and some bright spark said, "I've heard about these homemade nuclear fallout shelters, it might be one of them." Everybody laughed.'

JOHN SULLIVAN

'I had a few ideas about how to play Rodney, basing some of his uncomfortable body language on a friend's younger brother, who was a little awkward because of his age. There were other influences as well, of course. When it came to bringing the character to life in the first few episodes, though, it was pretty straightforward stuff – as it always is with John Sullivan's scripts because all the ingredients are there and you'd be pretty stupid if you couldn't make it work.'

NICHOLAS LYNDHURST

'THE LONG LEGS OF THE LAW'

Rodney isn't happy with Del, who suggested he comes along to make a foursome. The date, with a mother and daughter Del has known a long time, doesn't turn out as Rodney expected.

GRANDAD: What's the matter with you, Rodney? It sounds like a nice evening.

RODNEY: Grandad – when he said we was going out with a mother and her daughter I assumed that I'd be with the daughter. Instead of that, he drags me round every pub in the Old Kent Road holding hands with some old sort with a cough.

DEL: I thought it was a very romantic evening, Rodney.

RODNEY: Well it might have been for you, Del. For me the night air was filled with all the sensuous promise of a tour round the Sanatogen works.

....

We're introduced to greasy Sid's cafe in this episode, where Del and Rodney have just eaten breakfast and are paying.

SID: What did you have, Rodney?

RODNEY: Just me usual bacteria on toast.

'NO, NO, PAS DE BASQUE, PAS DE BASQUE.' (DEL)

....

Rodney is dating a policewoman; Del and Grandad can't believe it.

GRANDAD: I mean, Rodney going out with a policewoman. What are the neighbours gonna say? Why's he doing it to us, Del Boy?

At its peak, the Trotter family's adventures were watched by over 24 million people.

26

DEL: 'Cos he's kinky, ain't he. He's got what leading psychiatrists call a – 'a thing' about policewomen's uniforms.

> *Did you know?*
> Lennard Pearce, who played Grandad, came up with the idea of the character wearing pyjamas under his jumper and a trilby, originally borrowed from a friend.

GRANDAD: Well if that's all he wants can't we club together and buy him one?

DEL: He don't want to wear it, he wants the policewoman to wear it. Gordon Bennett, he may be perverted but he ain't dangerous!

'ASHES TO ASHES'

Feeling sorry for Trigger, the local road sweeper, who's attending his gran's funeral on his own, Del says he'll come along with Rodney and Grandad. At the house, before the funeral …

TRIGGER: Fancy a drink?

GRANDAD: No.

TRIGGER: (*To Rodney*) Dave?

DEL: Just a small large one, Trigger.

RODNEY: (*To Del*) Oi, don't you think this is the wrong time and place to be shanting it up?

Memories ...

'Everyone I know had someone at their school who didn't seem to be quite with you, or thought differently. We're all travelling on a train line, but he's over there on a different train holding a different view, taking the wrong attitude to things and not on the same wavelength.

'Trigger was a loyal guy and someone Del took under his wing. Del had great affection for him and wouldn't let anyone harm him in any way. That showed great loyalty: this man, Derek Trotter, who'd make money out of you if possible, had a real heart. It was a nice opportunity to show what Del was all about.

'I think Trigger ended up funnier than when he started. The actual decibels in terms of laughter he got were incredible. Sometimes you would just write, "Trigger enters", and the audience would start laughing as soon as he did just that – the character was that strong.'

JOHN SULLIVAN

Trigger wasn't the brightest star in the universe.

DEL: No, no, of course not. Eh, Trigger, what you reckon, eh? Would your gran like to think of us, standing around moping and mourning?

'THE TRUTH IS ONLY RELATIVE TO WHAT YOU CAN EARN FROM A LIE!' (DEL)

TRIGGER: Yeah, she'd have loved it. She was a miserable old cow!

'A LOSING STREAK'

Grandad tries to warn Del, who's gambling heavily, about the perils of the activity.

GRANDAD: Well, I were in a card school once where the cards was marked. I lost a fortune.

DEL: What, you knew they were marked?

GRANDAD: Oh yeah, I marked 'em … I was never much good at cards.

....

Del tries to persuade Grandad to loan him some money to feed his gambling addiction.

DEL: Come on, Grandad, lend us £100! I'll pay you back double. Now be fair, I've always been straight with you, haven't I?

Remember last month, when you said you was feeling the cold in bed, what did I do for you?

GRANDAD: You bought me an electric blanket.

DEL: Right. Give me that £100 and I'll put a plug on it for you.

Gambling was nearly the ruin of Del.

'NO GREATER LOVE'

A nervous Rodney arranges a date with an older woman.

IRENE: Well, how old are you?

RODNEY: Well, I'm not a kid if that's what you mean. I'm 23 and a half.

IRENE: That's what I mean. You're 23 and a half, and I'm older than you.

'APPELLATION BORDEAUX CONTROLÉE!' (DEL)

RODNEY: So?

IRENE: Well, doesn't it bother you?

Memories ...

'Sue Holderness and I hit it off from the beginning and have been chums ever since. She's an excellent character actress but we owe so much to John Sullivan.

'One of the great things about the first script I got in 1981 was that it jumped off the page and made me laugh. Actually, John's material has always made me laugh, including *Green, Green, Grass*. There are some terrific jokes and wonderful set-pieces, but laced throughout with great characterisation and brilliant plotting.

'Among my favourite episodes in *Only Fools* is "The Sky's The Limit". Boycie had a new satellite system so was using a remote control to show how good he was at all this high-tec stuff, plus Marlene had Tyler in a pram, there was a dog in the scene and I had all this dialogue! I thought it would be a nightmare but everything worked well.

'One of my favourite moments in the series was the famous Batman and Robin scene, where Del and Rodney turn up at a wake thinking they're attending a fancy dress party, much to Boycie's amusement, who ushers them through without telling them. It was a terrific situation to play and great writing.

'I don't mind Boycie overshadowing other work I've done. If you're in anything as good as *Only Fools* and *Green, Green, Grass* you're going to get identified; it's something you have to accept. Appearing in a popular series is a double-edged sword because it opens and closes doors. But for me it's great to have been involved in a series people love so much.'

JOHN CHALLIS (Boycie)

Boycie was a flashy, boastful kind of guy.

RODNEY: No, does it bother you?

IRENE: Well … no.

RODNEY: So where's the problem?

Later in the exchange

IRENE: Rodney, you sure you don't mind? People might stare.

RODNEY: Let them stare. That sort of thing don't bother me, Irene.

....

Marcus, a spiky-haired punk, walks in to the Nag's Head, passes pleasantries with Del and Rodney, before proceeding to the bar.

DEL: I bet he could pick up BBC2 on that hair.

'THE YELLOW PERIL'

Del describes their mother to Rodney, who died when he was an infant.

DEL: Our Mum was a wonderful woman. She had long blonde hair – sometimes. Every night you'd see her sitting at the bar in the Nag's Head with her simulated beaver skin – with her rum and pep in one hand, 20 Senior Service in the other. She looked like a lady – lots of people mistook her for a money lender.

RODNEY: Really?

DEL: Straight up. Of course, I was much younger then and didn't have much money, but every night she used to send me across two or three pints of light and bitter, or whisky if she was flush. That was Mum. Then come about ten o'clock she'd look over where I was sitting and she'd shout, 'Come on, Del Boy, get off home to bed – school in the morning!' That was the kind of woman she was, Rodney, concerned about our welfare.

RODNEY: Where was I, then?

DEL: Outside in the pram eating an arrowroot.

....

Del tells Rodney about how he promised their dying mother that he'd look after him – and he never lets him forget it, too.

DEL: 'Look after Rodney for me, Del Boy,' she said. 'Share everything you've got with him, try to make him feel normal …'

'I'M GOING BACK TO THE HOTEL TO HAVE A FIESTA.' (GRANDAD)

And that's what I have done. Half of everything I've got … I mean, fair enough, I've got nothing, but half of it's yours.

RODNEY: You'd give me half of everything? You'd nick the hole out of me last polo if I didn't keep me mouth shut.

Del has roped Rodney and Grandad into painting the kitchen of a local Chinese takeaway, much to Rodders' chagrin.

DEL: Here we are, nice little kitchen innit?

RODNEY: Nice little kitchen? This is the pits, Del Boy. This is the bloody pits. The whole place looks like an explosion in a dripping factory.

DEL: This is a working kitchen, Rodney. You've got to expect a little bit of fat to spill out of the pan every now and then.

RODNEY: So what period are we going to decorate it in, Del? Early bubonic, perhaps?

DEL: Yes, if you like. Look, don't worry about it, you've had all your inoculations haven't you?

'IT NEVER RAINS'

Del and Rodney are booking a holiday in the sun but want to leave Grandad at home.

RODNEY: We can't take him with us, Del, he'll cramp our style, won't he? I mean you could bring a bird back to the room, go to pour her a Sangria or something and find his false teeth in the glass.

Did you know?

John Sullivan wanted Chas and Dave to sing the song used for the theme tune. When they were unavailable, he recorded it himself.

....

Del is dreaming of moving abroad when they become millionaires!

DEL: When we become millionaires we'll move out – get a villa … get Grandad one of them little old folks' homes that they have out here.

RODNEY: What old folks' homes they have out here?

DEL: You know, we saw 'em in the holiday brochure. What d'they call 'em? Pensions!

'A TOUCH OF GLASS'

Del is always the eternal dreamer, but in a moment of realism, he assesses his life and it doesn't paint a pretty picture.

DEL: I deserve a bit of the good life, worked hard enough for it; I mean, I've always been a trier. Where's it got me? Nowhere, that's where it's got me. We live 'alf a mile up in the sky in this Lego set built by the council. Run a three-wheel van with a bald tyre. We drink in wine bars where the only thing's got a vintage is the guvnor's wife.

'HOMESICK'

Crime is rife on the Trotters' estate and Rodney wants to see a greater police presence so intends raising the matter at the tenants' meeting. Del informs Rodney about an incident involving Rita Alldridge.

DEL: Last Friday night she was indecently assaulted over by the adventure playground.

> ### Did you know?
> The original block of flats used to represent Nelson Mandela House was in North Acton, just off the Bollo Bridge Road. Later on, a block in Bristol was used.

RODNEY: No, did she report it?

DEL: Yeah, I saw her this morning, she'd just been down the police station.

RODNEY: Right, there you are you see, that's exactly the sort of thing ... hang on a minute, if this happened on Friday night, how come it's taken her till Wednesday to report it?

DEL: Because she didn't know she'd been indecently assaulted until this morning when the bloke's cheque bounced.

....

Trigger always calls Rodney 'Dave', so at the local tenant's meeting, Rodney asks why.

RODNEY: Trigger, why d'you call me Dave? My name's not Dave, my name's Rodney.

TRIGGER: I thought it was Dave.

'LA PLUME DE MA TANTE.' (DEL)

RODNEY: No, it's Rodney.

TRIGGER: You sure?

Memories . . .

'I can't remember why I got Trigger calling Rodney "Dave".
The first few times I did it, I wish I hadn't bothered because
nobody got it. The audience were so quiet. But when we
did it the next year, everyone caught on and it became a
regular thing.'

JOHN SULLIVAN

RODNEY: Yeah, I'm positive. I've looked it up on me birth certificate and passport and everything. It is definitely Rodney.

TRIGGER: Oh well, you live 'n' learn. So what's Dave, a nickname like?

RODNEY: No. You're the only one who calls me Dave. Everybody else calls me Rodney, and the reason they call me Rodney is because Rodney is my name.

TRIGGER: Oh well. I shall have to get used to calling you Rodney.

RODNEY: Thank you.

TRIGGER: (*Calls to chairman*) Here, Basil. You gonna get this meeting started? Me and Dave ain't got all night.

'HEALTHY COMPETITION'

Del has a close shave with a policeman while out on the street selling his wares. Later, he vents his annoyance on Rodney, who should have warned him.

GRANDAD: I mean, they are difficult to spot – with their size 18 boots and their pointed heads.

RODNEY: Why don't you shut your mouth you sarky old goat.

Did you know?
Ronnie Barker was instrumental in launching John Sullivan's writing career. Whilst playing Fletcher in *Porridge*, Barker agreed to read some sketches Sullivan had penned.

DEL: Oh, and that's another thing. What about last Friday then, when we were knocking out them Italian shirts. Listen to this one, Grandad. That wasn't just one copper you failed to warn me about, it was an entire squad car. I mean, it stood there by the kerb, all big and white with a red stripe running through it like a tube of Signal.

A last-minute look at the script during rehearsals.

RODNEY: Well, I didn't see it.

DEL: You didn't see it … you must have been a tiny suspicious when this ginormous great big jam sandwich pulled up next to you?

....

Rodney assesses his life and doesn't think he's achieved much to be proud of.

RODNEY: I am 24 years old, I have two GCEs, 13 years of schooling and three terms at an adult education centre behind me, right. And with all that, what have I become? I'm a look-out.

'YESTERDAY NEVER COMES'

Del thinks he's snapped up a Queen Anne cabinet, an antique which will earn him a packet. Rodney isn't so sure.

RODNEY: (*Examining the cabinet*) Hey, it's got woodworm.

DEL: That has not got woodworm.

GRANDAD: What's all them little holes then?

'THIS TIME NEXT YEAR WE'LL BE MILLIONAIRES.' (DEL)

DEL: Well I don't know. Maybe Queen Anne played darts. (*Banging the lift doors*) Where's these lifts? I'll tell you what, I'm considering letting the British Museum take a look at it.

RODNEY: Yeah? I'd let Rentokil have a go first.

DEL: You don't know nothing about antiques you, do you? I mean, dealers often put holes in items like these to give it that sort of 'distressed' look.

RODNEY: Distressed. Del, this thing looks panic-stricken.

....

Del thinks he's struck it lucky with scheming Miranda, not realising she's only after him for one thing – and it's not what Del thinks.

RODNEY: What d'you drag me in here for?

DEL: 'Cos I want your advice, Rodney, I think she fancies me.

RODNEY: Miranda?

DEL: Yeah.

RODNEY: Leave it out, Del, she's an intelligent woman.

Memories ...

'The trio of Grandad, Rodney and Del provided me with a young, naïve guy who was a little lost and not quite sure of the future, the middle-aged guy who was too old to be naïve but too young to be despairing and the older man who had seen it all and couldn't care less.

Buster Merryfield took up acting after a successful banking career.

'Having three characters is great because they can side against each other. Two would regularly team up against the other. When we lost Lennard [Pearce] I realised I needed to replace that third person – the older, more experienced man – so brought in the brother who we knew little about because he'd been abroad.

'I made him a sailor and whereas Grandad was lazy and wouldn't get out of his chair, his brother was full of energy and had a real history; it made a nice gear change. It took the character a series and a half to get accepted but it worked well in the end – and Buster was very good.

'I was involved in the casting of Grandad. Lennard entered Ray Butt's office with that lovely gruff voice. We'd seen other actors and you knew they were acting, whereas Lennard's performance was so genuine.

'He was a lovely actor and extremely nice man. My kids were young at the time and I'll never forget attending a parents' evening and finding the teacher confused; the kids had told her they had three grandfathers: my dad, my wife's dad and Grandad Trotter – they actually thought he was their grandad! A lovely man.'

JOHN SULLIVAN

'MAY THE FORCE BE WITH YOU'

It's hard work talking to Trigger, as Rodney finds out one day in the Nag's Head.

RODNEY: So, right, I said to her, I said, 'Bernice' … I said …

TRIGGER: That her name is it?

'HE WHO DARES WINS.' (DEL)

RODNEY: Yeah, Bernice! Yeah, Trigger, that's why I call her Bernice, you know.

TRIGGER: Right.

RODNEY: I said, 'Don't play with me, girl, 'cos you are playing with fire.' I said, 'Don't you dare try an' tie me down.'

TRIGGER: She's into all that, is she?

RODNEY: No, Trigger, I meant it in a, you know, spiritual sort of way. I mean she's not – no – see, 'cos I'm a free agent, Trigger. Wherever I might lay my hat, that's my home. That's the sort of guy I am.

TRIGGER: Yeah … you got a hat now then have you, Dave?

Relaxing at the Nag's Head after another busy day on the streets.

Memories ...

'The Nag's Head was just a name, although my brother-in-law held his wedding night at a pub called it. I liked the name, it sounds like a lovely old-fashioned London name. It was any pub I'd ever been in.'

'Denzil started as a nice, genuine guy who Del could control. He could almost hypnotise him and get him agreeing to anything. Denzil realised this but couldn't stop it happening.

'Paul [Barber] is a lovely actor. When Ray Butt suggested him for the part, we asked him to come and see us, and he was perfect. He wasn't an obvious comedy character. Del would feed off him more, but towards the end he was getting a lot of laughs.'

JOHN SULLIVAN

'WHO'S A PRETTY BOY?'

Del, Rodney and Grandad visit Denzil's house to discuss business.

DENZIL: I haven't seen you for ages, where have you been?

DEL: Well, you know me, here, there and everywhere – ducking and diving.

DENZIL: Rodney, you're looking good.

RODNEY: (*In cool voice*) Yeah!

DENZIL: He's cool, I like it. I tell you, if he wasn't so white I'd swear he was black.

DEL: Yeah, he is white ain't he?

DENZIL: He's the whitest man I've ever seen in all my life!

60

Memories ...

'My first episode was "To Hull And Back" in which I had to drive a 16-gear truck. Fortunately the real driver was in the cab, out of shot, when I crawled over the Humber Bridge. Creeping along in third gear was like driving a Ferrari in first on the M6!

'Playing Denzil helped my career and people often called me by the character's name. I'd be walking along the street with people shouting, "Denzil!" At first I didn't react because I didn't think they were talking to me, but I eventually got used to it.'

PAUL BARBER (Denzil)

Denzil (Paul Barber) was a close friend of Del and Rodney's.

'HAPPY RETURNS'

Del stops a boy, Jason, from running into the road. He later discovers that he's the son of a former fiancée. They start talking.

JASON: I've seen the bogey man!

DEL: Have you? What's he look like?

JASON: He's got a funny old hat and wears pyjamas under his mac.

DEL: That's not the bogey man, that's my grandad!

....

Del tells Rodney he was engaged to June, the mother of the little boy who was running into the road until stopped by Del.

RODNEY: When d'you meet her then?

DEL: 1964.

RODNEY: What and you've only just come round to see her?

DEL: No, I was engaged to her, soppy!

RODNEY: What, another one! Stone me, Del, you've been engaged more times than a switchboard, ain't yer?

....

Del bumps into Mickey Pearce at the Nag's Head

DEL: What you up to, Mickey?

MICKEY: I've just come from evening school. I'm learning Aikido.

DEL: Really? Go on then, say something.

MICKEY: Eh?

DEL: Say something in Aikido.

MICKEY: No, it's not a language, Del. It's a martial art. I had a fight with five blokes last night.

'YOU KNOW IT MAKES SENSE.' (DEL)

DEL: What was it, a pillow fight? Leave it out, you ain't got a mark on you, son.

MICKEY: That's because I wiped 'em all out with Aikido.

DEL: (*Sniffing the air*) Can you smell that? What is that? Sheep is it? It's cows? No, no, I know what it is, it's bullshit!

....

Del visits the gents' at the Nag's Head and sees Trigger. Del's worried but Trigger gets the wrong end of the stick and thinks he's desperate for the toilet.

TRIGGER: Alright, Del Boy?

DEL: (*Desperately pacing the floor*) No, I'm not alright, Trigger. I don't know what I'm gonna do. I just don't know what I'm gonna do!

TRIGGER: Hang on, Del Boy, leave it to me. (*Bangs on cubicle door*) Come on, hurry up, we've got an emergency out here!

....

When Del thinks June's little boy is his, he stops Rodney seeing June's daughter, just in case they're related. Rodney isn't happy when his brother announces the news.

DEL: Alright, Rodney. Come on, that's why I had to tell you, you see, 'cos this sort of thing it ain't allowed – it's … well, it's incense! Say you had got married to her – you can see what sort of confusion that would have led to, I would have been your father-in-law!

RODNEY: Bloody hell!

DEL: Yer mother-in-law would have been yer aunt, yer wife would have been your second cousin – gawd knows what that would have made Grandad: the fairy godmother I should think.

'STRAINED RELATIONS'

Grandad has died. After the funeral, Uncle Albert, who's going to become an important part of Del and Rodney's lives, enquires about staying a few days. Del's worried it'll turn into a long-term arrangement.

RODNEY: Uncle Albert might not be like that.

DEL: Oh leave it out, Rodney. You've heard him yourself when he was telling us about that time he came round the Cape of Good Hope – he was three months on the same wave!

'YOU NEARLY GAVE MY HEART A CONNERY, THEN.' (DEL)

66

Mike, the barman at the Nag's Head, asks Del about Uncle Albert.

MIKE: What is he, a relative or something?

> *Did you know?*
> Bearded Buster Merryfield only turned to acting after retiring from his role as a bank manager.

DEL: Nah – well yeah, I mean, he's a distant relative.

MIKE: He was telling me all about his wartime dramas. Torpedoed five times, dive-bombed twice. He's a bit of a jinx, ain't he?

DEL: Yeah. You know what his last job was don't you? He was entertainments officer on the *Belgrano*.

'SLEEPING DOGS LIE'

Del meets Boycie, then Marlene appears.

DEL: Hello, Marlene, my love.

MARLENE: Hello, sweetheart.

'YEAH, ALL THE LADS REMEMBER MARLENE.' (TRIGGER)

They kiss and Del touches her up

DEL: Wohoo!

MARLENE: Did you have a nice Christmas?

DEL: Oh triffic, yeah.

MARLENE: I had a dog.

DEL: Yeah, we had a turkey, same as every other year.

....

While Boycie and Marlene head for the Seychelles' sun, Del and Rodney agree to babysit their enormous dog, Duke.

MARLENE: Duke, this is your uncle Del and Rodney. He's lovely ain't he?

DEL: Triffic!

MARLENE: Take him for walkies first thing in the morning, once in the evening and then again last thing at night. When it's his bedtime you put a blanket over him and then you talk to him for a while.

DEL: You don't want us to bring his wind up?

MARLENE: No, he should be alright. And don't worry, he's house-trained.

RODNEY: But we live in a flat!

Memories ...

'Helping create Marlene was great fun. In the brief it said she was a dapper little Cockney woman. There wasn't much more than that, but it was clear from her history that she was a woman who stood out in a crowd. The idea of the bright-coloured skirt, high heels, stockings, suspenders, huge fur coat and hair was a joy to create.

'Everyone in the street expects me to be an old slapper like Marlene and are disappointed when they see me in jeans and t-shirt. I'm a disappointment to the fans because I don't sound or look like Marlene.

'But alarmingly, I'm finding my wardrobe is veering towards Marlene's; I've even bought the odd bit of leopard skin. Sad, isn't it?'

'They always say don't work with children or animals so it was alarming that my first and only scene – as far as I knew – was going to be with Duke, this huge dog. Fortunately, the dog and I struck up a profound friendship, he was terribly sweet.

'Over the years, we had four Dukes, so I don't think I ever worked with the first one again which is sad because I did rather fall in love with him, although he had bad breath and when he kissed me back, it wasn't as thrilling as it might have been.

'The only reason I was in the scene was because of the dog. It was mentioned regularly that all the boys remember Marlene so one had this wonderful picture of a terrible old tart from Peckham, like George Cole's "er indoors" in *Minder*. I think John considered keeping Marlene indoors so everyone could imagine this monstrous creature, but then he came up with the storyline involving the dog.

'So I thought the job was going to be just one scene. As I was pregnant with my first daughter, I regarded it as a nice job before giving birth. I had such a lovely time, though, that a bit of me wondered whether they'd have Marlene appearing again. Luckily, I didn't have to wait long.'

SUE HOLDERNESS (Marlene)

Marlene opens a hold-all to reveal huge steaks, etc.

MARLENE: In here his vitamin pills. One in the morning, before breakfast, not after.

BOYCIE: We've got a plane to catch, Marlene. Come on, kiss him goodbye.

MARLENE: Bye, Del, see you soon.

BOYCIE: For gawd's sake, the dog, Marlene!

MARLENE: Bye-bye, my little bubba-luba. I know Dooky's gonna miss his mummy, and mummy's gonna miss her little dookie-wookie wookie.

BOYCIE: Makes you wanna throw up, don't it?

'FROM PRUSSIA WITH LOVE'

Marlene and Boycie are desperate for a baby so Del, spotting the perfect opportunity for a little business, has the perfect solution. Rodney has befriended a homeless and pregnant 19-year-old student. When she indicates she wants to put the baby up for adoption, Del decides Boycie and Marlene could adopt the child. As always, his plan backfires.

BOYCIE: (*Looking into the cot, he sees the baby is black*) The deal's off is it? Too bleedin right it's off.

DEL: What are you talking about? What? How?

RODNEY: That's the other thing I meant to tell you out there. You see, Spencer's mummy and daddy came over in 1956 from the West Indies.

They squabbled and fought, but Boycie and Marlene's love remained strong.

When an unwanted baby appears on the scene, Del has a bright idea.

75

MARLENE: Well, it don't bother me, Boyce.

BOYCIE: Leave off, Marlene. The baby's brown.

MARLENE: So is Duke.

BOYCIE: But I ain't claiming to be Duke's father.

ALBERT: There is a likeness, though.

BOYCIE: Just shut it.

MARLENE: We could say it's a throw-back.

BOYCIE: For gawd's sake, Marlene. I might be able to con people into buying my cars. I might be able to convince 'em that you conceived and gave birth in seven days flat, but how the hell am I gonna persuade 'em that my grandad was Louis Armstrong! You ain't heard the last of this, Del Boy!

Memories ...

'This remains my favourite episode, even after all these years, because it has all the elements that John Sullivan does so well; he makes you care about the characters. This scene brought the house down, although I had to leave the baby. Within three seconds of the audience weeping with joy, they were weeping with real sorrow at Marlene's predicament. That's what Sullivan does so well, make an audience laugh and cry within a fraction of a moment. Many people wrote to me, sympathising about Marlene's situation.

'People still refer to me as Marlene but I don't mind. Some actors aren't known for anything, so it's a great thrill to be remembered for such a joy. Thanks to Marlene, I've never had more than three months out of work.'

SUE HOLDERNESS (Marlene)

Del's adoption plans backfire big time.

'TEA FOR THREE'

Trigger's niece, Lisa, is spending a few days in Peckham. Del recalls her mother.

DEL: She was a fair sort – pig-ugly, but a fair sort. I nicknamed her Miss 999 you know 'cos I only phoned her in an emergency.

Did you know?
Original costume designer, Phoebe De Gaye, was keen for Del Boy to have a perm, which were popular back then. David Jason, however, wasn't so keen.

'A ROYAL FLUSH'

Del is out trading.

DEL: Come along now, ladies, make the neighbours jealous. Only the finest steel goes into the making of this premier cutlery.

MAN: Yeah, but how do we know that?

DEL: (*Removes a knife*) Run your wrist gently down the blade, you'll soon find out.

....

Rodney is dating Vicky, who's terribly posh.

VICKY: Where do you lunch?

RODNEY: Lunch? Oh, I usually go down to the Greasy Thumb.

VICKY: The Greasy Thumb?

RODNEY: No, it's Sid's Caff really, we just call it the Greasy Thumb – out of affection.

VICKY: May I join you for lunch?

RODNEY: You? In the Greasy Thumb? Oh I don't think you'd like it, Victoria. It's all steam and bacteria – it's 'orrible.

....

Vicky gets her way and they dine at Sid's establishment.

RODNEY: The egg, bubble and beans twice.

SID: (*Hands him two plates*) There you go, Rodney. Don't forget your tea, son. (*Collects someone's order from a hatch and calls*) Two of dripping toast! Bacon, egg and one slice.

....

Albert has cleaned the Reliant van's interior with disinfectant but the smell is making Rodney feel nauseous.

ALBERT: They could perform an operation on the floor of this van.

Memories . . .

'I worked on building sites before I started writing and met plenty of miserable café owners. I wanted a grumpy guy with a cigarette in his mouth in the series and Roy Heather came in and was very good. As the show progressed, I started writing the part up and getting Sid more involved.

'When poor Ken McDonald passed away, I'd already written much of the series with Ken heavily involved. I had to make a sudden change and as Sid had run his own catering business, he seemed the obvious choice to step up and run the pub in Mike's absence.'

'When I introduced the Reliant Regal, it represented something else missing in Del and Rodney's lives. Their mum had died and father had left them and even their van had something missing. I thought giving them a three-wheeler van was a nice idea. Del would have got it when he was 16 or 17, when you could drive such a vehicle on a motorbike licence. We had several vans during the series and they were surprisingly reliable.'

JOHN SULLIVAN

RODNEY: That's what's making me feel ill, the pong of that disinfectant. It's like being a Dettol delivery man! Disinfectant and exhaust fumes. When we gonna get rid of this van?

DEL: Why, what's wrong with it?

RODNEY: What's wrong wi ... Look in your mirror. The Fire of London couldn't have made that much smoke.

ALBERT: It's just burning off a bit of carbon, Rodney.

RODNEY: Leave off! Half the estate's suffering with bronchitis 'cos of this van.

'OH, MON DIEU, MON DIEU.' (DEL)

DEL: This is the thoroughbred of three-wheelers. There's a highly-tuned machine under that bonnet.

RODNEY: This van is like one of your birds. It drinks too much, makes funny noises and is old enough to know better.

Several Reliant Regals were used during the sitcom's lifetime.

'THE FROG'S LEGACY'

Trigger's niece, Lisa, gets married. At the reception, Del is chatting to Boycie and Marlene. They discover they've both bought her tea sets.

BOYCIE: I shouldn't worry, Marlene, there'll be no comparison. We got ours from Royal Doulton, they most probably got theirs from *Dalton's Weekly*.

DEL: (*To Rodney*) He's something else, ain't he? He's got more front than Southend.

'DATES'

Trigger walks into the Nag's Head.

MIKE: 'Ere, talk of changing luck, look at this.

Trigger enters wearing a brown two-piece suit, purple shirt, orange tie, colourful V-neck jumper and carrying flowers.

TRIGGER: Alright, Boycie?

BOYCIE: Well, I was.

'THAT IS FATE, RODNEY, UNISON OPPORTUNAIRE.' (DEL)

The pompous second-hand car dealer relaxes with a cigar and tipple.

Memories ...

'Boycie is the longest-running character I've played and definitely one of the best. He didn't have any class but thought he did because he had money; he was a good example of the nouveau riche of that period.

'I thought I'd failed when I started receiving lots of fan letters because he was supposed to be an awful character yet so many people loved him; he seemed to inspire a lot of affection, but then that's the great watching British public for you.

'Part of Boycie's image was smoking cigars. In 1997, there was great consternation because I had to smoke cigars in pub scenes and had just given up cigarettes. Thankfully, it didn't make me return to smoking.'

JOHN CHALLIS (Boycie)

MIKE: (*Places drink on counter*) There you go, Trig, there's a Scotch, mate.

TRIGGER: How did you know I wanted a Scotch?

MIKE: 'Cos if I was dressed like that, I'd want a Scotch.

> *Did you know?*
> John Challis worked as an estate agent before becoming a professional actor.

Del meets Raquel on a blind date. They have agreed to rendezvous at the train station. Del presents a bouquet of flowers to her.

RAQUEL: You shouldn't have gone to all this expense.

DEL: Mais oui, mais oui. Well, I've booked a table at my favourite restaurant – if that is alright with you?

RAQUEL: Oh yes, sounds lovely.

Del met his wife-to-be, Raquel, on a blind date.

The working relationship of Nicholas Lyndhurst and David Jason couldn't have been better.

Memories . . .

'The idea of Del using French phrases came from a car trader I'd worked for, who used Latin phrases. We never knew if they were correct because we didn't understand them, but he thought he was impressing us. When it came to Del, the Common Market was upon us and I thought that he, like the car trader, would have picked up a few little phrases to try and impress people: what he says, though, is either out of context or rubbish. Of course, Rodney realised that the only people Del was impressing were the morons in the Nag's Head.'

JOHN SULLIVAN

DEL: (*Gesturing towards cab rank*) Your carriage awaits.

RAQUEL: Thank you. This is a bit like *Brief Encounter*, isn't it?

DEL: You reckon?

RAQUEL: That's my favourite film.

DEL: Mine as well.

RAQUEL: Really?

DEL: Yes, I loved the bit at the end when the big spaceship comes down and all the little martians come out.

RAQUEL: That's *Close Encounters*.

DEL: Yeah. Loved it.

'YUPPY LOVE'

The Trotters are considering buying their council flat.

RODNEY: Alright, think of it from a business point of view, eh? I mean this flat is in a wonderful position. It's 15 minutes from the West End, it's 15 minutes from the motorway.

ALBERT: And 15 minutes from the ground.

'LOVELY JUBBLY.' (DEL)

DEL: You're right. I never thought of that! (*Starts writing in his filofax*) That's a very good selling point. I'm gonna make a note of that. That could put a few grand on.

Memories ...

'The relationship between Boycie and Marlene was hugely successful. Quite a few people I've known seem to get by on the strength of their conflict. The chances are the audience know people like that, too. In fact, I get letters from many people saying: "I know people in the village …"

'Having worked in the car trade I've known people like Boycie. They all had lovely houses, and if they had £10 more in their pocket they'd class themselves better than you.

'When I thought Boycie was becoming unbearable, I gave him a weakness, a fallibility in the shape of Marlene with this terrible reputation; it was a nice way of pricking Boycie's balloon of pomposity. Marlene was his Achilles' heel.

'John was used in *Citizen Smith* as a plainclothes policeman and I'll always remember the way he acted in a court scene. I was already thinking about Boycie and spotted the pomposity, aloofness I was looking for. I said I'd be in touch, although John thought he'd never hear from me again. About three years later, I phoned him.

'I only saw Sue's involvement being the one-off scene in "Sleeping Dogs Lie". But when I watched the rushes she was so good I had to use her again.'

JOHN SULLIVAN

Del, sporting his new yuppy image, tries impressing two girls in a wine bar.

DEL: Oh – it's good to unwind, innit?

MARSHA: Sorry?

DEL: I say, after a hard day in the City, it's good to unwind.

DALE: I imagine it must be very tiring.

DEL: Tiring? I'm cream crackered and that's no lie. Well, I've been up since six this morning trying to talk to a bloke in New York.

MARSHA: Why didn't you use a telephone?

The girls burst out in squeals of laughter. Del can't see the joke and can't see they are taking the rise out of him.

DEL: No, I've got a phone an' all that. No, I mean, it's just a long and stressful day in the old commodities market. It ain't all champagne and skittles. Oh no – buying, selling, making billion-pound decisions. It's a git of a journey home an' all.

DALE: What exactly do you buy and sell in the commodities market?

As usual, Del's attempt to impress the girls fails dismally.

DEL: Oh, you know, this and that, whatever's going, you know. Iron ore, sugar beet. I made a killing today on olive oil. Gawd knows what Popeye'll say when he gets home. (*Laughs uproariously*)

....

Rodney meets Cassandra in the foyer of the local education centre.

CASSANDRA: Hello!

RODNEY: (*Looks up and reacts, surprised and delighted*) Oh! (*Realises this was too enthusiastic and cools it*) Hi!

Did you know?
Playing Cassandra was Gwyneth Strong's first taste of situation comedy.

CASSANDRA: Sorry to interrupt you.

RODNEY: Oh what? No, it's alright, just some computer data I've to put into a program.

CASSANDRA: It looks very complicated.

RODNEY: Well, yeah, it does look difficult, but it's no problem … My name's Rodney.

'EVERYTHING'S CUSHTY!' (DEL)

CASSANDRA: Cassandra.

Rodney and Cassandra shake hands.

RODNEY: Oh Cassandra. That's a lovely name.

CASSANDRA: Thank you. Um, I just wanted to say …

RODNEY: I'm glad we've bumped into each other 'cos I was trying to find a way of saying hello to you and I think it's really, you know, sort of liberated for you to make the first move.

CASSANDRA: Move? No, you don't understand. You've taken my coat!

RODNEY: (*Looks at the coat he's holding. We now see it's a woman's coat*) Oh, I am so sorry.

Memories . . .

'In terms of enjoyment and pleasure, Cassandra has got to be one of my favourite jobs of all time, especially when I consider all the lovely friendships I made through playing her.

'I definitely liked Cassandra as a character because she was written as a "modern woman" in terms of wanting to keep her career going, even when she settled down. As an actress, I'd always wanted to play someone like that, so I liked that part of her.

'Another reason I warmed to the character instantly was because I loved the show so much. My whole family watched it. Cassandra was a very natural person to play. Before her, a lot of the roles I'd played were fairly aggressive, working-class parts in the theatre; Cassandra was a total contrast, which made it even more interesting.'

GWYNETH STRONG (Cassandra)

Gwyneth delivered an adroit performance as career girl Cassandra.

CASSANDRA: It's OK. They're very similar; it's an easy mistake to make. This one's yours.

RODNEY: Well, how d'you know it's mine?

CASSANDRA: It's got your name written in it.

'DANGER UXD'

Del has invested in a video recorder.

ALBERT: What is it?

DEL: What is it? It's a videotape recorder. It's got a little computer and everything. When you go on your holidays this thing will record all your favourite shows for you.

ALBERT: Amazing.

DEL: Nothing but the best.

ALBERT: How does it know you're on holiday?

DEL: You send it a postcard, don't you? You programme its little computer, you daft old …

'CHAIN GANG'

Del arrives at the One Eleven Club.

TRIGGER: Alright, Del Boy?

DEL: Wotcher, Trig.

TRIGGER: No Dave?

DEL: Yeah, he's coming down later. He's bringing that bird of his – what's her name … Cassandra.

TRIGGER: He's going a bit serious, ain't he?

DEL: No, birds always blow him out after a couple of weeks. That boy's been blown out more times than a windsock.

Trigger (Roger Lloyd Pack) became hugely popular with audiences.

'THE UNLUCKY WINNER IS ...'

Del walks in on Rodney and Cassandra, who are enjoying a kiss and cuddle.

DEL: Oh what are you two doing? You look as though you're waiting for your case to come up.

RODNEY: We've just been, em ... discussing art, that's all.

DEL: Oh isn't it funny that every time he discusses art with someone their buttons come undone.

Life's archetypal street traders prepare for another day.

Memories ...

'David Jason and Nick Lyndhurst worked together brilliantly. There was an instant chemistry. When we were casting, I wanted them to be the only people in Peckham who believed they were brothers.

'Ray Butt wanted Jim Broadbent as Del, but having a big Del and small Rodney wouldn't have worked. The things Del said and did to his younger brother would have been seen as bullying. A small Del and a big Rodney would work, though.

'John Howard Davies secured Nick Lyndhurst, whom he'd seen in *Going Straight* with Ronnie Barker. I was happy with that. When Ray Butt suggested David Jason for Del, I was keen to chat with him. I'd never seen him play a dominating character, he'd always played the fool. I wanted to be sure he was right.

'One day, David phoned me at home and said: "Am I doing this or not?" I replied: "Let's have a drink." We met in the BBC Club and went to Ray's office to chat. David was too big an actor for me to ask him to read but he wanted to. Nick Lyndhurst happened to be in John Howard Davies' office and popped in for a drink with us. They ended up doing a scene together, after which I said to Ray: "Let's get some champagne, we've done it!" It was so obvious they'd work well together. David was such a live wire while Nick was laid back. The chemistry was so good and intelligent.'

JOHN SULLIVAN

'SICKNESS AND WEALTH'

Del talks to Dr Meadows at the hospital while being examined because of severe stomach pains.

DEL: Anyway, how comes they've put you in charge?

DR MEADOWS: It was an accident, really. I just happened to be talking to some colleagues when the name Derek Trotter cropped up. So I asked if I could read your GP's report and have a look at your tests. I was amazed. I found myself reading about this non-smoking, teetotal, celibate vegetarian health freak. I thought, 'Can this be the same Derek Trotter that I know and begrudgingly admire? That uptight, wheeling-dealing, pina colada lout? The Castella king, the curry connoisseur? The same man who has lived his life on nervous tension, fried bread and doubtful women?

DEL: And was it?

DR MEADOWS: Yes, it was. Why did you lie to your GP, Del?

DEL: 'Cos she's a doctor.

'GORDON BENNETT!' (DEL)

DR MEADOWS: I don't understand.

DEL: Well, you never tell doctors the truth, do yer? Otherwise
you'll end up in hospital.

'LITTLE PROBLEMS'

Rodney has just got married. Del and Rodney share an emotional exchange.

DEL: Are you off then, bruv?

RODNEY: Yeah, going in a minute.

DEL: Just wanted to … er … just wanted to say, Rodney, that I'm really very proud of you. You've got it all now, ain't you? New job, new flat, new wife, new life.

RODNEY: Yeah. We had a few good years, eh?

DEL: Some good times.

RODNEY: Some right laughs, eh?

Memories . . .

'I like using scenes like this to introduce some humanity. It's all very well bouncing gags off each other but it's nice every so often to have these moments. When Rodney left and Del was standing on his own, I let David, the director and Mick Hucknall do the work, singing about holding back the tears and the years. All this time Del had taken the mickey out of Rodney, putting him down. Now his younger brother is going, he's lost.'

JOHN SULLIVAN

DEL: And a couple of tears. But that's all part of it. I just wish that Mum …

RODNEY: Oh no, shut up! You'll have me going.

They now just look at each other. It's almost as if one of them's emigrating. Rodney now embraces Del. Del shouts in pain.

DEL: Oohhh.

RODNEY: What's wrong?

DEL: I got a bit of a bruise. I don't know how I got it.

CASSANDRA: Goodbye, Del, and thanks for everything.

DEL: That's alright, sweetheart. Listen, will you do something for me?

CASSANDRA: What?

DEL: Be gentle with him.

CASSANDRA: Oh shut up!

'THE JOLLY BOYS' OUTING'

The lads are off on a jolly to Margate and Sid is miffed as to why he wasn't asked to make the sandwiches.

SID: Oi, I wanna word with you.

> 'BOYCIE WOULD SCALP YOU IF DANDRUFF HAD A GOING RATE.' (RODNEY)

DEL: Yeah, what is it, Sid?

SID: I own a café, right?

DEL: Yeah, right, so what?

SID: So, why didn't you ask me to make the sandwiches?

'IT'S BOEUF À LA MODE, AS THE FRENCH SAY.' (DEL)

DEL: Well, the explanation is simple. We intend to eat them.

> ### Did you know?
> Roy Heather, who played Sid the café owner, turned to acting late in his working life, having worked as a warehouse manager for 14 years.

Sid transferred his questionable culinary skills from the greasy cafe to the local pub.

'RODNEY COME HOME'

Raquel, who's back from the States, pops in to see Rodney, who's head of the computing section at a printing company.

RAQUEL: A couple of weeks ago I was over in America, having a great time when suddenly I thought …

RODNEY: Hold on a minute, you were in America?

RAQUEL: Didn't Del say?

RODNEY: No.

RAQUEL: Oh it was wonderful. We were doing this tour of *My Fair Lady* down the east coast. I was the flower-seller.

RODNEY: Cosmic!

RAQUEL: Yeah, alright – it was very cheap and cheerful but I was seeing the world and getting paid. We did Atlantic City, Miami, New Orleans. Then suddenly I get this sort of urge to come home.

RODNEY: What, to Del?

RAQUEL: Yes, to Del.

RODNEY: I wouldn't come home from New Orleans to see Del. I wouldn't come home from the New Forest to see Del!

RAQUEL: Oh, you don't see him the way I do. He's lovely.

RODNEY: There are many words I could use to describe Derek Trotter but lovely is not one of them … how's the old sod keeping?

RAQUEL: He's fine. He seems – I don't know – quieter than when I first met him.

RODNEY: Del? Raquel, some years ago Del joined a monastery and took a vow of loudness.

Rodney and Cassandra aren't getting along too well.

RODNEY: Me – childish? You're the one who's got to start growing up a bit, Cassandra. When are you gonna realise that you've got a marriage – you've got a home – and you've got *me*.

CASSANDRA: Oh, I never forget that, Roddy.

'WILL YOU GIVE IT A REST, ALBERT, YOU'VE DONE MORE BLEEDIN' WHINING THAN A SPIN-DRYER.' (DEL)

RODNEY: I never see you. You just use this flat like a base camp. You zoom in and out of here like a bluebottle with the runs. I've had double-glazing salesmen spend more time in here than you.

CASSANDRA: Well, whatever turns you on.

RODNEY: And what's that supposed to mean?

CASSANDRA: Look, Rodney, I like to keep myself occupied.

RODNEY: But you're always out – on your own.

Memories ...

'As the series progressed, it reached a stage where we realised we couldn't continue having Del going to discos and chasing young totty. It was time he acted more his own age and found a permanent relationship. But I didn't want to simply bring a female character in and find we were stuck with her. So in the episode 'Dates' I introduced Raquel, whom Del met via a dating agency. I thought we'd see how it went – a kind of pilot episode for the future. But Tessa was so good and the public loved her. We received so many letters, and I was stopped in shops by people asking about Raquel, so the following Christmas we brought her back permanently.

'We then brought Cassandra in for Rodney. Then along came the babies, all of which helped move the series along. We started showing all the things a family goes through: a funeral, wedding, birth – and it worked.'

JOHN SULLIVAN

CASSANDRA: Because you never want to go anywhere with me. I've asked you before to come to badminton but you always refuse.

RODNEY: Because I don't relish the idea of spending an entire evening whacking a dead budgie over a net.

Rodney finally ties the knot in a tear-jerking episode.

'THE SKY'S THE LIMIT'

Del announces to Uncle Albert that Raquel isn't sleeping in Rodney's old room, she's sleeping with him. With Rodney back at the flat, it seems an opportune moment to raise the subject.

ALBERT: Where'd he sleep then?

DEL: He slept in his old room.

> **'I USED TO MISS MY DAD – TILL I LEARNT TO PUNCH STRAIGHT!' (DEL)**

ALBERT: I thought Raquel slept in there?

DEL: Er … no!

ALBERT: Where'd she sleep then?

DEL: (*Mumbles*) I don't believe him! She slept … er … somewhere else.

ALBERT: Oh I see. Where?

DEL: Gordon Bennett! If you could raise your voice by half a decibel they might be able to hear you in the Doodoyne!

ALBERT: You mean she slept with you?

DEL: Well … yes! Here, don't you go saying nothing to her about it.

ALBERT: Don't she know, then?

DEL: I mean, it might embarrass her.

ALBERT: No wonder you're looking so chirpy! (*Laughs*)

DEL: That laugh. Sounds like someone trying to push-start a Lada!

Memories …

'John Sullivan is a genius when it comes to comedy. Every age group can watch a Sullivan script and have a gloriously happy time. You're moved by the characters and grow to love them, as if they're members of your own family.

'It's alarming because I'm so closely associated with Marlene I sometimes think I'm turning in to her! A lot of the time I say things and think, "That's completely Marlene"; I'm also starting to dress like her. I appeared on *Loose Women* recently and the night before chose what clothes to wear. When I asked Mark, my husband, whether he thought the outfit was all right, he replied: "Yes, if you want to look like Marlene!"'

SUE HOLDERNESS (Marlene)

'STAGE FRIGHT'

Del is trying to be a real yuppy.

ALBERT: I couldn't get in touch with yer. You've been out all morning, I thought you might have popped home for elevenses.

DEL: How many times I gotta tell you, Unc? Elevenses is for wimps. I'm out there on that yuppy tightrope, nerves on red alert. A beta-blocker and a dream, that's me. I eat on the move, mobile phone in one hand, a Pot Noodle in the other.

> ### Did you know?
> John Sullivan chose Peckham as the Trotters' home town because when he was growing up it was the toughest place he knew.

Tony Angelino, an entertainer, is singing at the Riverside Club. He can't pronounce his Rs.

TONY: You're not alone with your pwejudice. We've got sexism, wacecism, sizeism and ageism. Well, I'm a victim of pwonunciationism! I've got a good voice. I've got a good style. I've got a perfect tone. But just because I pwonounce my Rs differently fwom the west of you I can never be a star. Just because of my pwonunciation you've dumped me.

'WHERE DO YOU THINK I WORK, THE METAPHORICAL OFFICE OR SOMEWHERE?' (DEL)

'THREE MEN, A WOMAN AND A BABY'

At The Nag's Head, the regulars discuss what Del's baby is going to be called.

MIKE: What name have they decided on?

TRIGGER: If it's a girl they're calling her Sigourney after an actress, and if it's a boy they're naming him Rodney after Dave.

MIKE: Brilliant!

Memories . . .

'When I received my first *Only Fools* script, Trigger was described as someone who looked like a horse. That was all I had to go on when it came to deciding how to play the character; not much, I know, but I knew it was a promising sidestep if I could play someone like that. I also realised from the start that it was clearly a good script. Obviously no one could foresee just how successful the programme would become, but it was certainly a show with plenty of potential.

'I can't remember when I realised the show was really taking off, but suppose it was when the episodes increased to 50 minutes. The stories became epics, possessing a degree of grandeur. It showed the strength of the characters because not many half-hour shows can be expanded in that way.'

ROGER LLOYD PACK (Trigger)

130

....

The baby is born. In the delivery room, Del is standing next to Raquel, who's holding the new arrival.

DEL: It's a baby, Raquel.

RAQUEL: I've been wondering what that swelling was.

DEL: We've got ourselves a lovely little baby.

RAQUEL: I know. I love you.

DEL: I love you too, sweetheart.

Love soon blossomed for Del and Raquel. (Tessa Peake-Jones)

Memories ...

'When I first appeared on the show I was very nervous. Up until that point, I wasn't very familiar with the programme because I'd been doing lots of theatre, so tended not to be around much in the evenings. Therefore, I didn't have any preconceptions about what I was going into. There are always nerves with any part because you really want to do it well, but I was even more nervous than usual because I loved the character and the script so much; I was desperate to do my best. Any new job is like starting at a new school, with lots of people you've never met before; but I needn't have worried because I felt at home almost immediately.'

TESSA PEAKE-JONES (Raquel)

....

Del talks to his new-born son.

DEL: Oh, you are such a lovely little boy, you really are. You've got a mummy and daddy who think you're the most precious thing in the whole wide world. You've got a lovely family around you. Yes, you have, look. You've got your Uncle Rodney to play with. Great Uncle Albert. He'll tell you about all the places in the world he's been to – and sunk. And there's me. And you're gonna have all the things your daddy couldn't afford. 'Cos I've been a bit of a dreamer, you know. Yeah, I have. You know I wanted to do things, be someone, but I never had what it took. But you're different, you're gonna do all the things I always wanted to do and you're gonna come back and tell me about them. Tell me if they're as good as I thought they would be. You're gonna have such fun. You are, and when you get the hump, 'cos you're bound to get the hump sometimes, I'll muck about and make you laugh. 'Cos I've mucked about all my life, and I never knew the reason why until now. This is what it's all about. I was born for this moment. Oh we're gonna have such fun, we are, you mark my words. This time next year we'll be millionaires.

'MOTHER NATURE'S SON'

Rodney isn't happy with his lot.

CASSANDRA: What's the time?

RODNEY: It's time for us to emigrate or at least discuss the advantages of a suicide pact.

CASSANDRA: And how are we feeling this morning?

RODNEY: Great! How else could I feel? I'm thirty-one years of age and I work for Trotters Independent Traders.

CASSANDRA: There are lots of people who'd give their right arm to be in your position.

RODNEY: I know, but they're all tucked up safe and sound in their padded cells.

'FATAL EXTRACTION'

Raquel isn't happy with her life with Del.

RODNEY: So how's life treating you?

RAQUEL: How's life treating me? D'you mean besides him coming in at all hours of the morning, spending every spare hour with his mates down the pub and wasting our money in that casino?

RODNEY: Yeah.

'OH YES, PETIT SUISSE.' (DEL)

RAQUEL: I'll give you an example of how life's treating me, Rodney. Have you seen what's inside my wardrobe?

RODNEY: No.

135

RAQUEL: Well, not to put too fine a point on it, the only times my clothes look fashionable is when I'm watching UK Gold. Now, a short while ago Del happened to mention that he had a contact in the rag trade. This fella could get the very latest fashion *and* all the top designer labels. Christmas was approaching, Del asked me what I'd like. 'Anything you want, sweetheart, just name it.' So I said I wouldn't mind a little number by Bruce Oldfield. (*She holds up album cover*) He got me *Tubular Bells*!

RODNEY: That's Mike Oldfield.

'HEROES AND VILLAINS'

Trigger is a proud man. At Sid's café he tells everyone about his award, a proud moment in his family's history.

BOYCIE: Trigger, you haven't got a family history. You were created by a chemical spillage at a germ warfare plant somewhere off Deptford High Street.

TRIGGER: Maybe. But I still feel proud.

RODNEY: So what exactly is the award for?

TRIGGER: For saving the council money. I happened to mention to her [Councillor Murray, head of finance and facilities at the town hall] one day that I've had the same broom for the last 20 years. She was very impressed and said have a medal. 20 years. Long time, Dave.

> ### Did you know?
> David Jason worked as a mechanic and electrician before he switched careers and became an actor.

RODNEY: Yeah, I know. It's two decades, innit?

TRIGGER: I wouldn't go that far, but it's a long time.

The sniffy Boycie, played by former estate agent John Challis.

Memories . . .

'I played a disreputable policeman in an episode of *Citizen Smith*, a character based loosely on a chap I knew at my local pub. I used a few of his extraordinary characteristics. Afterwards, John said he liked the character and would try and put him in a series one day. I didn't think any more about it until asked to record an episode of *Only Fools*, this time playing a secondhand car salesman.

'I didn't receive any instruction on how to play Boycie, so as it was the same producer/director and writer, I changed him a bit from the character in *Citizen Smith* but basically he possessed the same characteristics, plus what I knew about secondhand car salesmen. And it worked.'

JOHN CHALLIS (Boycie)

'MODERN MEN'

It's a tragic time for Rodney and Cassandra when they lose their baby. Rodney visits the hospital with Del.

DEL: You didn't let anyone down, sweetheart. And don't blame yourself. You tell her, Rodney. This time next year – go on, tell her.

RODNEY: Yeah I will. (*Aimed at Del*) Look, I think maybe this'd be a good time for us to be on our own to discuss a few things.

DEL: Yeah, I think you're right, bruv. Cassandra, me and Rodney are gonna pop outside for a little chat.

RODNEY: No, I meant me and Cassandra should be on our own.

Memories ...

'A cousin of mine had had two miscarriages. Somebody said you never look at the man's point of view. The woman is shattered but what does it do to the bloke? So I thought I'd take a crack at it; I showed the script to a few people and they thought it was pretty good. Everyone in the scene was brilliant but Nick, you knew you'd get an incredible performance.'

JOHN SULLIVAN

DEL: Of course. Yes, right. I'll see you later, Cassandra. And ... (*Doesn't know what to say*) You know ... I'll wait for you outside, Rodders.

Del exits.

CASSANDRA: (*Cries*) I lost our baby.

'THIS TIME NEXT YEAR WE'LL BE BILLIONAIRES!' (DEL)

RODNEY: I know. I can't leave you alone with anything, can I? (*He smiles at her. She smiles back through her tears*) We're gonna get over this, Cass, and we're gonna win. And d'you know why? It's because we are strong – very strong. Things are gonna get better and better and better for us. Or as Del would say, betterer.

'TIME ON OUR HANDS'

Rodney is in the garage itemising all the bits and pieces the Trotters' company has acquired over the years.

RODNEY: Well, I'm gonna make a note of everything. And I'm gonna chuck a lot of this junk out.

DEL: Now you be careful, Rodney. Remember, one man's junk is another man's treasures.

'LET'S FACE IT, DEL, MOST OF YOUR FRENCH PHRASES COME STRAIGHT OUT OF A CITROËN MANUAL.' (RODNEY)

RODNEY: Derek, we have got a pile of Showaddywaddy LPs in the corner under a tyre for a Triumph Herald and an artificial limb. They are not gonna make big news on *The Antiques Roadshow*!

DEL: Those LPs are collectors' items.

RODNEY: Well, let's find a one-legged Showaddywaddy freak and flog 'em to him. And if he turns up in a Triumph Herald we've had a result!

....

The Trotters finally become millionaires, but it's not as much fun as Del anticipated.

RODNEY: So how are you?

DEL: Oh, couldn't be better, bruv. It's wonderful – everything's coming up roses.

RODNEY: Alright, what's wrong?

DEL: It's all so easy now. All my life I've dreamt of becoming a millionaire; of having a Rolls Royce and a big house in the country and jetting off to the Caribbean and all that.

RODNEY: Well, you've got it.

DEL: I know. But it's not the way I thought it would be. You see, the dreaming and scheming and chasing and trying – that was the fun part, you know. It was dangerous, impossible – it was like Columbo sailing away to find America, not sure whether he was gonna fall off the edge of the world. That's how I used to feel.

RODNEY: Well, you fell off a couple of times, didn't you?

DEL: Once a month regular. But now I've found it – I've got what I was searching for – the hunt is over, and what do I do now? Learn to play golf?

TEST YOUR KNOWLEDGE

As Del would say, 'He Who Dares Wins', so pull up your chair, sharpen your pencil and try your luck with this *Only Fools* quiz – you know it makes sense!

1. What was Del and Rodney's mother's Christian name?

2. Who sang the songs heard during the opening and closing credits?

3. In the episode, 'The Yellow Peril', what did Del persuade Rodney to paint?

4. What kind of business did Cassandra's father run?

5. Which well-known actor played Detective Inspector Slater in the series?

6. In 'The Jolly Boys' Outing' which coastal resort did the lads visit?

7. What comes crashing down around Del and Rodney in 'A Touch of Glass'?

8. What does T.I.T.C.O. stand for?

9. What is Del's son called?

10. Before meeting Del, what job did Raquel have?